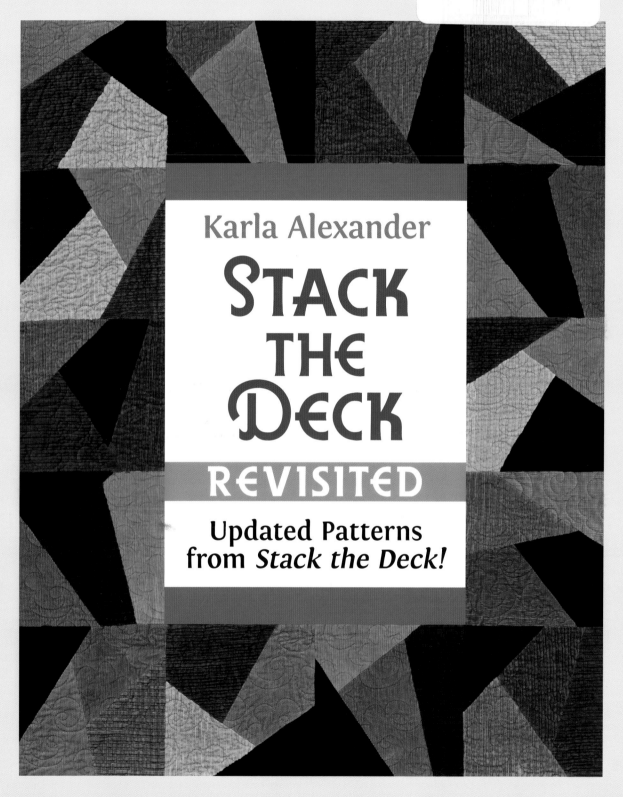

Karla Alexander

Stack the Deck

REVISITED

Updated Patterns from *Stack the Deck!*

Martingale®
& COMPANY

DEDICATION

To my son Kelly Collins

ACKNOWLEDGMENTS

Thank you to the talented team at Martingale & Company for the great work and for allowing me to write another stack-the-deck book. Thanks to E.E. Schenck for providing a stack of wonderful batik fabrics for me to sew my way through. I also extend a special thank-you to my long-arm quilter, Dalana Prunk of Heart to Heart Country Quilting. Dalana quilted most of the quilts in this book and did a superb job.

Last but not least, thanks to my family for their awesome support. My son Kelly Collins helped with the following quilts: "Goin' Green," "Asian Fusion," "Summer Solstice," and "My Favorite Cords." He lent his time and hands, sewing alongside me late into the evening many nights. He also voiced his opinion when I strayed from idea to idea. Thank you, Kelly, for keeping me on track!

Stack the Deck Revisited: Updated Patterns from *Stack the Deck!*
© 2010 by Karla Alexander

That Patchwork Place® is an imprint of Martingale & Company®.

Martingale & Company
19021 120th Ave. NE, Ste. 102
Bothell, WA 98011-9511 USA
www.martingale-pub.com

Credits
President & CEO: Tom Wierzbicki
Editorial Director: Mary V. Green
Managing Editor: Tina Cook
Design Director: Stan Green
Technical Editor: Ellen Pahl
Copy Editor: Marcy Heffernan
Production Manager: Regina Girard
Illustrator: Robin Strobel
Cover & Text Designer: Stan Green
Photographer: Brent Kane

Mission Statement
Dedicated to providing quality products and service to inspire creativity.

Printed in China
15 14 13 12 11 10   8 7 6 5 4 3 2 1

Library of Congress Cataloging-in-Publication Data is available upon request.

ISBN: 978-1-60468-031-7

CONTENTS

ꟷNTRODUCTION

Through trial and error, I've discovered that there is never just one way to go about sewing a project. In fact, I'm quite sure I found a new way to do just about anything anyone ever tried to teach or show me!

I really enjoy designing quilts and writing books because they provide the opportunity for me to continue discovering endless new ways of doing things.

When I wrote my first book, *Stack the Deck!*, I definitely shared "my way," and as a result, I've had the pleasure of teaching hundreds of students to stack, cut, shuffle, and sew their own decks.

With *Stack the Deck!* now out of print but still in demand, I decided it was time for an update. Originally the plan was to simply reproduce the quilts in new fabric for an updated look. I tried very hard to stick with the plan; however, stacking, cutting, shuffling, and sewing decks is so much fun, and I got so caught up with the possibilities that before I knew it, I had changed most of the original quilts using new ideas and variations. I couldn't help sharing a new spin that had evolved over the past several years. I've gained an enormous amount of knowledge from teaching, and new inspiration seemed to sprout with every new quilt.

The basic idea of stacking the deck is to begin with squares—what could be easier? Once the squares are cut, you'll stack them into decks, slice them, shuffle, and sew. Here are the basic rules for stacking the deck.

1. **Stack** squares of assorted fabrics into a deck, like playing cards.
2. **Slice** the deck into crazy shapes, following a block cutting and sewing guide for the chosen quilt project.
3. **Shuffle** the pieces in each stack. (See page 7 for details on shuffling.)
4. **Sew** the pieces in each layer of the deck together to make Crazy blocks. Trim the resulting blocks to the required size.

It's fun, it's easy, and it's fast. My goal is that the quilts in this book will inspire you—that you'll have fun and make the projects uniquely yours by discovering your own free spirit in the process. I hope my passion becomes yours as you create you own Crazy quilts with my method. So, get a little crazy and enjoy!

—*Karla Alexander*

Getting Started

To make your project a positive experience, be sure to review "Tools and Supplies" below as well as "Making the Crazy Blocks" on page 6. If you haven't ever tried this style of piecing, sharpen your blade and get ready. It's a lot of fun! Every quilt you make from this book will be original, different from one to the next due to the unique cuts for each block. Relax and enjoy the journey.

TOOLS AND SUPPLIES

Purchase the best tools you can afford, as good tools yield good results, making the process more enjoyable.

Rotary cutter. You will use a rotary cutter to slice through many layers of fabric. It's important to begin each project with a sharp new blade for your cutter. I prefer the medium-sized 45 mm rotary cutter; however, a large 60 mm rotary cutter is nice with its larger blade. Choose whichever one feels best to you.

Cutting mat. My favorite size is 24" x 35"; however, if your space is limited, a 17" x 23" mat will work fine.

Acrylic rulers. A 6" x 24" ruler is great for cutting long strips, and square rulers are helpful for cutting large squares and trimming up pieced blocks.

Sewing thread. Use neutral colors for piecing your blocks. I like to use good-quality, 100% cotton thread.

Quilting thread. I like to use a variety of good-quality thread, from cotton to silky rayon, in colors and textures that enhance the pieced quilt top.

Spray sizing. I am a huge fan of spray sizing. It helps fight distortion and keeps the edges of my pieces nice and crisp.

FABRIC CHOICES

One of the most exciting parts of beginning a new project is choosing the fabrics. It can also be the most challenging. For the Crazy blocks, I've found it helpful to choose fabrics in groups of three. For example, if I choose a print with a white background or with white designs, I will choose at least two more to go along with it. Working in groups of three helps distribute colors and prints throughout your quilt, so that one particular print or color doesn't stick out. I always apply my "10-foot rule" before making my final choices.

The Crazy blocks can be made from a wide assortment of colors and prints, just like any traditionally pieced scrap quilt. They can also be more controlled, with a planned color scheme or theme-related fabric, such as holiday or juvenile prints. For example, you could make a quilt entirely out of pastels to create a baby quilt.

Before beginning any project, I always check my stash to see if there is something I can use. The quilts in this book make it especially easy to toss in an extra replacement square or two so long as it plays well with what you already have selected. Adding more fabric to the mix spices things up! If you look closely at the photographs, you'll probably detect that some of the quilts contain more fabrics than the instructions call for. I challenge you to go through your stash and use up your leftovers!

The 10-Foot Rule

Make it a habit to preview all fabrics before inviting them into your quilt. If you're at the quilt store, stand the bolts of fabric side by side; then back up approximately 10 feet and take a look. If you're at home working from your stash, fan the fabrics out across your design wall or lay them out across the top of a couch so the fabrics can be viewed vertically. Do the fabrics contrast well with one another? If one fabric appears to jump out from the rest, it may need another companion; use three instead of one. However, make sure that each fabric in the group of three, while similar in color or design, is different enough from the others so they don't appear to be a single piece of fabric.

One of my favorite tools for evaluating fabric and layouts is a simple door peephole. Looking through a peephole distances you from your fabric choices and helps determine if you have a "jumper" (a fabric that jumps out from the rest) or if you have too many fabrics that blend together so that you're unable to tell the difference from one fabric to the next. The peephole is simply a tool to achieve the same result as my 10-foot rule.

Making the Crazy Blocks

This book uses my Stack the Deck technique, which gives you the advantage of using many different fabrics and unusual shapes without having to do any math or detailed cutting. If you want more blocks than the pattern calls for, simply cut a square or rectangle to equal the number of blocks desired. It's also easy to check your stash and recover a few favorite pieces from a small amount of fabric. As long as you can cut it into a square or rectangle as required in the quilt pattern, you can usually use it. I love that option!

STACKING THE DECK

Once you cut the required number of squares or rectangles, stack the number of pieces indicated in the pattern right side up for rotary cutting. Alternate colors as directed for each individual quilt. Stack the squares or rectangles as neatly as you can, keeping the edges even. Make sure you haven't duplicated the same fabric in any one deck. Keep in mind that the top fabric will eventually be moved to the bottom of the deck, so it's a good idea to make sure that sufficient contrast exists between the top and bottom fabrics. I like to lay out my deck, spreading the layers on top of one another to make sure I have no duplications and that I like the mix in the deck.

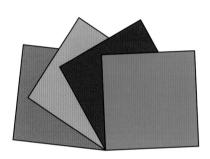

The Block Cutting and Sewing Guide

The directions for each project include a block cutting and sewing guide, which is similar to a template. It's a reduced version of the block and gives you the size to cut the original square. The cutting order for slicing the stacked decks is given numerically in red on the block segments. The sewing order is listed numerically in blue following the cutting number.

Use the red numbers as your guide when cutting the deck of stacked fabric into segments. Use the blue numbers as the order for shuffling and sewing the pieces back together.

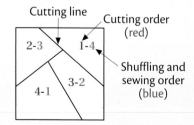

Cutting line
Cutting order (red)

2-3   1-4

4-1   3-2

Shuffling and sewing order (blue)

Block cutting and sewing guide
Cut size: 11" x 11" (size to cut original square)
Trimmed size: 8" x 8" (size to cut sewn square)

SLICING THE DECKS

Once your decks are neatly stacked, you'll use your rotary cutter and ruler to cut the deck in pieces as directed. You can slice the deck freehand by simply referring to the cutting diagram with each quilt, or you can make a cutting guide out of paper.

To cut freehand, refer to the cutting guide diagram and use a chalk marker to draw the cutting lines directly onto the top fabric in the deck. Brush any lines away if you don't like the outcome and redraw until you do. Vary the lines from deck to deck, always paying attention to the number of cuts and the style in each illustration.

To make a paper cutting guide, use a piece of paper the same size as your squares and draw the cutting lines as close as possible to those on the diagram. Don't worry if yours don't look exactly like mine; the whole idea behind this method is that you will create your own cuts. Fold the paper back on the first cutting line and place it on top of the deck of fabric squares. Carefully cut right next to the fold. Move the stack of new cuts out of the cutting zone and place them on another piece of paper, placing and orienting them the same as the original square. Continue folding and cutting until all the cuts have been made. Once your deck is sliced and placed on the other sheet of paper, it's time to shuffle. See page 7 top left.

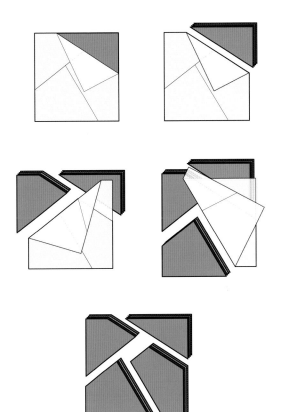

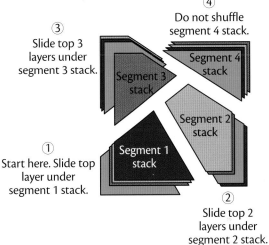

4. Do not shuffle the segment 4 stack. The last segment stack in the deck does not get shuffled. For decks with more pieces, continue shuffling each segment stack in numerical order in the same manner, removing from the top and repositioning to the bottom the same number of fabrics as the number of the segment stack you are shuffling, until all but the last segment stack have been shuffled.

④ Do not shuffle segment 4 stack.

③ Slide top 3 layers under segment 3 stack.

Segment 4 stack

Segment 3 stack

Segment 2 stack

Segment 1 stack

① Start here. Slide top layer under segment 1 stack.

② Slide top 2 layers under segment 2 stack.

Continue with the instructions for shuffling and sewing to complete the blocks. Then make any notes on the original folded template such as whether you liked the cuts, how to move a cutting line over, etc. Of course you can use the paper again, and you can also reverse the block by placing the template upside down on your next deck. I usually vary my cutting lines a little with each deck. I strongly suggest slicing and sewing one deck at a time. This way you have the opportunity to make changes as desired along the way.

SHUFFLING THE DECKS

Shuffling the deck is always the same process, regardless of how many layers or segments there are. And, no matter how many segments you cut, you shuffle each stack in the deck only once. Refer to the illustration below as you review the shuffling instructions. Work with one numbered segment stack at a time. When shuffling, use the blue numbers. The shuffling order is the same as the sewing order.

1. Remove the top layer of the segment 1 stack and place it on the bottom of the stack.

2. Remove the top two layers from the segment 2 stack and place them on the bottom of the stack.

3. Remove the top three layers from the segment 3 stack and place them on the bottom of the stack.

PREPARING A PAPER LAYOUT

I can't stress the importance of this step enough. It will help keep your deck in order while sewing, help prevent mistakes, and give you the opportunity to keep a record of each deck. Write any useful information or notes about cutting or sewing on the paper as the blocks are completed.

After shuffling, arrange the segment stacks on a piece of paper and pin each stack to the paper. Be sure to pin through all layers, keeping the fabrics in the exact order and layout in which they were shuffled. The pins will keep the segments in order; I also add a safety pin to the top layer of segment stack 1 (blue number 1). This will help to keep the pieces in the correct order when sewing the segments together. Once the segments are secure, trace around the segment shapes with a pencil. The lines will create a handy reference so that you can keep the pieces in order and sew them together correctly. Keep the segment stacks pinned to the paper until you're ready to sew.

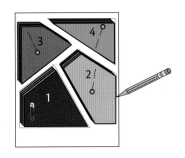

SEWING CRAZY BLOCKS

To determine where to begin sewing first, number the segments by following the order given in blue in the block cutting and sewing guide for the project you're making. For most blocks, the sewing order is the exact opposite of the cutting order. For instance, the last segment sliced will be segment 1 for sewing. The next-to-the-last piece is segment 2, and so on. The very first segment cut will be the last sewn and has the highest blue number. Once you've determined the sewing order, use a pencil to note the number on the paper, under the appropriate stack.

Be sure to keep the segment stacks in their shuffled order while sewing; otherwise you'll end up unintentionally duplicating a fabric within a block. After you chain piece all layers of segments 1 and 2 together, layer 1 always needs to be returned to the top of the stack, then the second layer, and so on. It's easy to reverse the order while ironing or clipping the pieces apart, so I rely on the safety pin in the top layer of the stack to keep the correct order. When you begin sewing again, you'll automatically know the combined pieces are in the right sequence if the safety pin is on top of the stack.

1. Unpin stacks 1 and 2 and peel off the top piece from each. Flip piece 2 onto piece 1 with right sides facing and sew them together. Without breaking the thread, sew pieces 1 and 2 from the next layer together. Continue to chain piece each layer until all segments 1 and 2 are sewn together in pairs.

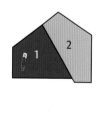

Chain stitch segments by flipping segment 2 onto segment 1. Continue sewing remaining segment pairs without breaking the thread between. Press.

2. Press the seam allowances to one side, clip the units apart, and restack them carefully in their original order; the safety pin should always be on the top.
3. Unpin stack 3 and sew segment 3 to the units you just made, right sides together, chain piecing as before.
4. Press, clip apart, and restack in the original order.
5. Continue adding segments in numerical order until all have been added.

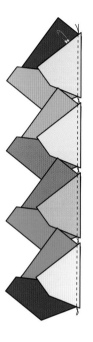

Continue adding new segments (in numerical order) to each combined unit. Press.

TRIMMING

The Crazy blocks in this book are all free-form cut; no ¼" seam allowances were added to the segments. When two segments are sewn together, they'll shrink approximately ½" and will always be shorter than the next segment you add. After pressing the seam allowances, you'll see the uneven edges. You can remedy this excess by what I call "following the inside passage." Trim the excess fabric using a rotary cutter and ruler by following the inside edge (passage) and angle of the smallest piece. You can also trim using scissors. Just remember to keep the segments in order as you trim.

After your blocks are completed and carefully pressed, place a square rotary-cutting ruler on top of the finished blocks and trim to the size specified in the project instructions.

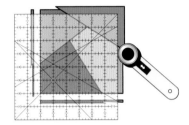

OTHER CRAZY-BLOCK STYLES

In addition to the basic Crazy block described above, you'll find a number of different block styles in the projects. Some blocks are cut crisscross style, resulting in blocks that have two sides of different color or value; these may resemble either a half Log Cabin block with random strips or a half-square-triangle unit. Some blocks are two sided, or "split." The first cut splits the block into two separate pieces; those pieces are then cut and assembled separately. The split block is then sewn together again after each side has been pieced. Other blocks are cut and reassembled into multiple units; you'll need to sew two or more segments together into one unit before adding it to the next segment or unit. Sections that need to be sewn together first are indicated with hash marks. See above top right.

joining split blocks

When sewing a split block together, trim the inside passage on each half before sewing them together. Carefully align the two halves of the block so that when stitched together they'll roughly create a square. The outer edges of the block may not align when you're sewing, but when you open up the block, it will more or less be a square rather than a rectangle. Press the seam allowances to the side in

Basic Crazy block

Crisscross block   **Diagonal crisscross block**

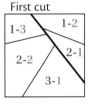 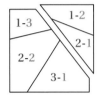

Split block

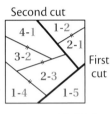 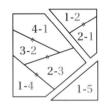

Multiple-unit block

either direction. Then square up the block as instructed in "Trimming" on page 8.

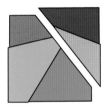

Align left and right sides to
create a square, not a rectangle.

VARIATIONS

Enjoy the process. Many of the projects in this book allow for variations. I encourage you to create your own work; I hope my designs will help you along your way. Allow your quilt to evolve as you go. Change a design by using different colors, adding borders, or even adding more blocks. I like to compare the quilts in this book to making soup! Keep adding to the mix until you're pleased.

Finishing the Quilt

Once all your blocks are complete, it's time for the layout. Arrange your blocks in rows according to the project instructions (or use your own arrangement). Play with the blocks—twist, turn, and substitute—until you're satisfied. I try to separate identical prints so that they don't end up next to each other in the finished quilt. View your arrangement from a distance using my "10-foot rule" (page 5) to check the visual balance.

Join your blocks into rows, matching the seams between the blocks. Press seam allowances in the opposite direction from row to row so that opposing seams butt against each other. Join the rows of blocks into sets of two rows, and then sew the sets together.

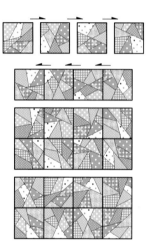

ADDING BORDERS

Some of the quilts in this book do not have borders. I chose this option because I truly believe a border or borders should make a quilt better and more beautiful, not just bigger! So if you find an awesome print that will make a borderless quilt look more fabulous, go for it and add a border.

1. Refer to the cutting directions for each quilt project and cut the required number of border strips.
2. Remove the selvages and sew the border strips together end to end to make one long strip. Press the seam allowances to one side.

3. Fold the long border strip in half lengthwise, matching short ends. Vertically center the folded border directly under the quilt top. Make sure the border and the quilt top are smooth without any wrinkles or pleats. Trim the doubled border strip even with the edges of the quilt top.

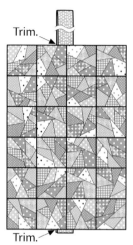

Trim border strip even with quilt top and bottom.

4. Mark the halfway point of the border length and quilt top with a pin. Pin the borders to opposite sides of the quilt, matching center marks and ends. Sew the borders in place, easing in any fullness. Press seam allowances toward the borders.
5. Repeat steps 3 and 4, centering the border strip horizontally under the quilt top, to cut and add the top and bottom borders.

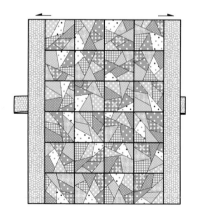

Trim border strip even with quilt sides.

LAYERING AND BASTING

Once your quilt top is completed, layer it with the backing and batting. The quilt batting and backing should always be at least 4" to 6" larger than the quilt top. Piece the backing with either a horizontal or vertical seam to make the best use of your fabric. Press the seam allowances to one side. Baste with safety pins for machine quilting or with thread for hand quilting. Quilt as desired.

BINDING

I prefer a double-fold, straight-grain binding. I preview my choices by placing a folded edge under the quilt top, peeking out just enough so that it shows me how the binding would look.

1. Trim the batting and backing even with the quilt top.
2. Refer to the cutting list for each individual project and cut the required number of binding strips.
3. Remove the selvages and piece the strips right sides together with diagonal seams as shown to make one long binding strip. Trim the seam allowances to ¼", and press the seam allowances open to reduce bulk.

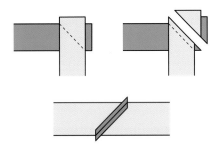

4. Fold the strip in half lengthwise, wrong sides together, and press.
5. I always use my walking foot when attaching binding. Beginning about 18" from a corner, place the binding right sides together with the quilt top. Align the raw edges. Leave a 10" tail and use a ¼" seam allowance to sew the binding to the front of your quilt. Stop sewing ¼" from the first corner and carefully backstitch two or three stitches. Clip the thread and remove the quilt from the machine.

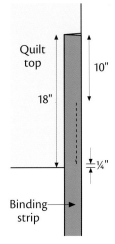

6. Rotate the quilt 90°, fold the binding up, creating a 45° angle, and then back down, even with the second side of the quilt. A little pleat will form at the corner. Resume stitching at the folded edge of the binding. Continue stitching the binding to the quilt, mitering each corner as described.

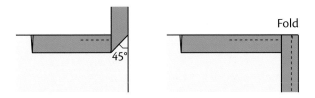

7. When you're approximately 10" from the starting point, stop sewing and remove the quilt from the sewing machine. Fold back the beginning and ending tails of the binding strips so that they meet in the center of the unsewn portion of the quilt edge. Finger-press the folded edges.

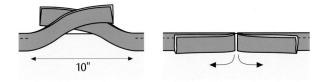

8. Unfold both ends of the binding and match the center points of the two finger-pressed folds, forming an X as shown. Pin and sew the two ends together on the diagonal of the fold lines. Trim the excess binding ¼" from the stitching line. Finger-press the new seam allowances open and refold the binding. Finish sewing the binding to the quilt.

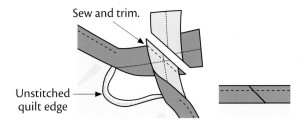

9. Fold the binding over the edge of the quilt to the backing, making sure to cover the machine stitching. Hand sew the binding in place, mitering the corners as you go.

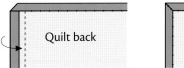

GOIN' GREEN

Using Crazy blocks as a background for all kinds of appliqué is a lot of fun. In this case, we appliquéd two sizes of open squares inside the larger framed blocks. To create an environmental theme, we chose bright lime green batiks .

fabric tips

Choose a mix of batiks in light to medium greens. I chose batiks that somewhat blended together because I wanted to use the blocks as a fractured background for the appliquéd frames. Of course, the quilt would be just as stunning in your favorite color, whether it's blue, red, or purple.

MATERIALS

2½ yards of black batik for appliquéd frames, block borders, inner border, and outer border

¼ yard *each* of 7 green batiks for blocks

⅝ yard of medium green batik for block borders

¼ yard of light green batik for middle border

⅝ yard of fabric for binding

3¼ yards of fabric for backing

57" x 71" piece of batting

⅔ yard of 17"-wide fusible web

Chalk marking pencil

CUTTING

From *each* of the 7 green batiks, cut:

1 strip, 8" x 42"; crosscut each strip into 5 squares, 8" x 8" (35 total)

From the medium green batik, cut:

13 strips, 1¼" x 42"; crosscut into:
    34 rectangles, 1¼" x 7½"
    34 rectangles, 1¼" x 6"

From the black batik, cut:

14 strips, 1¼" x 42"; crosscut into:
    36 rectangles, 1¼" x 7½"
    36 rectangles, 1¼" x 6"
5 strips, 2" x 42"
6 strips, 6" x 42"
1 rectangle, 18" x 26"

From the light green batik, cut:

5 strips, 1¼" x 42"

From the binding fabric, cut:

6 strips, 2½" x 42"

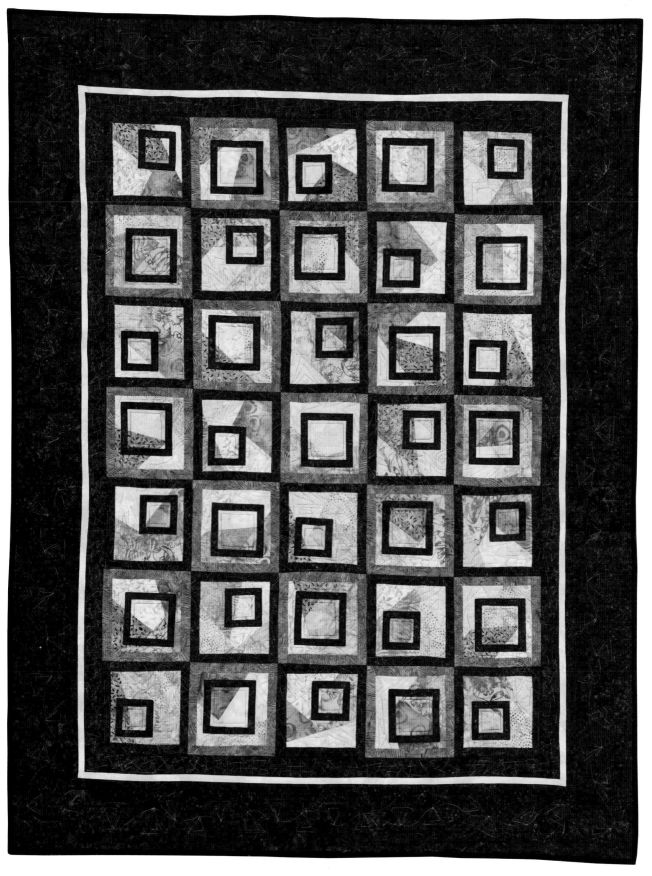

Finished quilt: 51" x 65" • Finished block: 5½" x 5½" • Blocks needed: 35 four-segment basic blocks

MAKING THE BLOCKS

Refer to "Making the Crazy Blocks" on pages 6–9 for details as needed. Vary the number of A and B blocks as you prefer.

Cut size: 8" x 8"   Trimmed size: 6" x 6"
Block A

Cut size: 8" x 8"   Trimmed size: 6" x 6"
Block B

Block cutting and sewing guide

1. Arrange the 8" squares into 7 decks of 5 squares each. Each deck should contain 5 different fabrics. Cut, shuffle, and secure each deck with a pin through all layers until ready to sew.

2. Make 35 four-segment whole blocks. Trim the blocks to 6" x 6".

3. Separate the blocks into two piles, one with 18 blocks and one with 17.

4. Sew 1¼" x 6" black batik rectangles to the sides of the 18 blocks. Press seam allowances toward the black batik. Sew 1¼" x 7½" black rectangles to the top and bottom of each block; press.

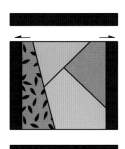
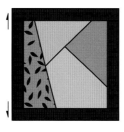

5. Repeat step 4 to add the green rectangles to the remaining 17 blocks.

6. Iron the 17" x 24" piece of fusible web to the wrong side of the 18" x 26" black batik rectangle, following the manufacturer's instructions. From the fused fabric, cut 18 squares, 4" x 4".

7. Measure in ½" along all sides of the 4" fused fabric square and draw a square using the chalk marker. Measure and draw a second square ½" smaller than the first. Use your rotary cutter and ruler to make a cut on one drawn line; then use scissors to complete the cutting all the way around the first square. Repeat to cut the smaller frame.

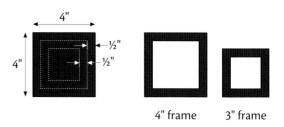

4" frame   3" frame

8. Position and fuse the 4" frames in the Crazy blocks with green borders approximately ½" in from two sides as shown. Position and fuse the 3" frames in the Crazy blocks with black borders approximately ½" in from two sides as shown.

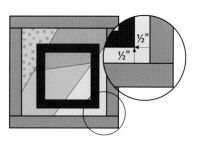

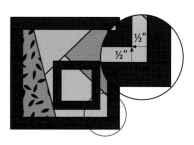

ASSEMBLING THE QUILT TOP

1. Arrange the blocks into seven horizontal rows of five blocks each. Alternate the blocks with green borders and the blocks with black borders, referring to the quilt photo on page 13 for placement. Turn the blocks until you're satisfied with the layout.

2. Pin and sew the blocks together in horizontal rows. Press the seam allowances in alternating directions. Sew the rows together and press the seam allowances in one direction.
3. Sew the strips for the inner border together to make one long strip. Press the seam allowances open. Repeat with strips for the middle and outer borders.
4. Trim to size and sew the inner-border strips to the quilt top, following the directions in "Adding Borders" on page 10. Press the seam allowances toward the border strips.
5. Add the middle and outer borders in the same manner as the inner border.

FINISHING YOUR QUILT

Refer to "Finishing the Quilt" beginning on page 10 as needed.

1. Divide the backing crosswise into two equal panels, each approximately 58" long. Remove the selvages and sew the pieces together along a long edge to make the backing. Press the seam allowances to one side.
2. Layer the quilt top with the batting and backing, keeping the backing seam parallel to the short edges of the quilt top. Baste the layers together using your favorite method.
3. Hand or machine quilt as desired.
4. Trim the backing and batting even with the edges of the quilt top and use the 2½"-wide strips to bind the quilt.

Asian Fusion

I can never resist the beauty and intricacy of Asian fabrics. Of course with all the selections, it's hard to choose just a couple of prints, so a Crazy quilt with 12 prints seemed like a great choice!

fabric tips

I chose strictly Asian fabrics in a variety of colors for this quilt. Each of the 12 different block fabrics included two or more colors as well as asymmetrical designs to help blend all the prints together. Choose the fabric for the setting triangles and border carefully as it will become the predominant color of your quilt in the end, regardless of the colors in the blocks.

MATERIALS

2 yards of teal print for setting triangles and outer border

⅜ yard *each* of 3 multicolored red prints for blocks

⅜ yard *each* of 3 multicolored black prints for blocks

⅜ yard *each* of 3 multicolored blue prints for blocks

⅜ yard *each* of 3 multicolored gold prints for blocks

⅜ yard of black print for inner border

⅔ yard of fabric for binding

4⅝ yards of fabric for backing

64" x 85" piece of batting

CUTTING

From *each* of the 12 multicolored prints, cut:

2 squares, 11" x 11" (24 total)

5 or 6 squares, 4¼" x 4¼" (64 total)

From the teal print, cut:

3 squares, 12¼" x 12¼"; cut the squares into quarters diagonally to make 12 large setting triangles

2 squares, 6¾" x 6¾"; cut the squares into quarters diagonally to make 8 small setting triangles

2 squares, 6½" x 6½"; cut the squares in half diagonally to make 4 corner setting triangles

7 strips, 6½" x 42"

From the black print, cut:

6 strips, 1¾" x 42"

From the binding fabric, cut:

8 strips, 2½" x 42"

Finished quilt: 57½" x 78½" • Finished block: 7½" x 7½" • Blocks needed: 24 five-segment split blocks

MAKING THE BLOCKS

Refer to "Making the Crazy Blocks" on pages 6–9 for details as needed. Vary the number of A and B blocks as you prefer.

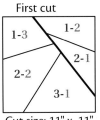

First cut

Cut size: 11" x 11"   Trimmed size: 8" x 8"
Block A

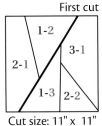

First cut

Cut size: 11" x 11"   Trimmed size: 8" x 8"
Block B

Block cutting and sewing guide

1. Arrange the 11" squares in four decks of six each. Each deck should contain six different prints. Cut, shuffle, and secure each deck with a pin through all layers until ready to sew.

2. Make 24 split blocks. Trim the blocks to 8" x 8".

3. Arrange three Crazy blocks and four 4¼" squares as shown to make a jumbo block. Sew the 4¼" squares together to make two two-patch units. Press seam allowances toward the darker fabric. Sew the two upper Crazy blocks together; press seam allowances to one side. Sew the two-patch units to both sides of the lower Crazy block. Press the seam allowances toward the two-patch units.

  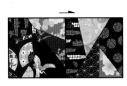

 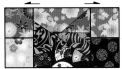

4. Pin and sew the upper portion to the lower portion to create the jumbo blocks. Press the seam allowances toward the two-patch units. Make eight jumbo blocks.

Make 8.

ASSEMBLING THE QUILT TOP

1. Arrange the blocks and large teal print setting triangles in diagonal rows as shown in the quilt diagram on page 19. Move and rotate the blocks until you're satisfied with the arrangement. Try to arrange the blocks so that identical prints are not side by side. Note that the setting triangles were cut larger than needed and will be trimmed later.

2. Use the remaining 4¼" squares to fill in the spaces along the edges of the layout. When you're satisfied with the arrangement, pin and sew the squares into six four-patch units and four two-patch units. Press seam allowances for the two-patch units toward the darker fabric. For the four-patch units, press the seam allowances for the two-patch sections in opposite directions; then press the final seam allowances to one side. Replace in the layout.

3. Add the four teal corner setting triangles and the eight small setting triangles to the quilt layout and look through a door peephole or use "The 10-Foot Rule" (page 5) to check the balance of colors.

4. Sew the rows together in sections to create units as shown in the quilt diagram and press as directed by the arrows. Join the units. Add the corner setting triangles last. Press the seam allowances toward the corners.

5. Trim and square up the edges of the quilt, making sure to leave at least a ¼" seam allowance beyond the corner point of each block.

6. Sew the strips for the inner border together to make one long strip. Trim to size and sew to the quilt as directed in "Adding Borders" on page 10. Press the seam allowances toward the border. Repeat with the strips for the outer border and press.

FINISHING YOUR QUILT

Refer to "Finishing the Quilt" beginning on page 10 as needed.

Quilt diagram

Summer Solstice

Fabrics with brilliant colors were the inspiration for this quilt. The overall quilt design evolved as each block was turned and moved throughout the layout. The layout possibilities are almost endless when you treat the blocks like a half-square-triangle unit with one dark half and one light half.

fabric tips

The blocks for this quilt are made of two contrasting colors and values. I chose light golds and greens for the light side and reds and oranges for the dark side. I included several different fabrics in each color. Preview fabric choices as you add them to the mix. They need to look good together as well as add visual interest with print design and texture.

MATERIALS

⅜ yard *each* of 8 red and orange prints for the blocks

⅜ yard *each* of 8 gold and light green prints for the blocks

⅞ yard of red orange print for the setting triangles

⅝ yard of fabric for binding

3½ yards of fabric for backing

60" x 82" piece of batting

CUTTING

From *each* of the 16 prints for the blocks, cut:

1 strip, 11" x 42"; crosscut into 4 squares, 11" x 11" (64 total)

From the red orange print, cut:

6 squares, 12" x 12"; cut each square into quarters diagonally to make 24 triangles

From the binding fabric, cut:

7 strips, 2½" x 42"

MAKING THE BLOCKS

Refer to "Making the Crazy Blocks" on pages 6–9 for details as needed.

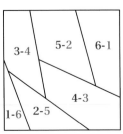 

Cut size: 11" x 11"   Trimmed size: 8" x 8"

Block cutting and sewing guide

Finished quilt: 53½" x 75¾" • Finished block: 7½" x 7½" • Blocks needed: 56 six-segment diagonal crisscross blocks

1. Arrange the 11" squares into 10 decks of six squares each. There will be four extra squares. Each deck should contain six different fabrics; alternate the red orange with the gold/green prints. Cut, shuffle, and secure each deck with a pin through all layers until ready to sew.

2. Make 60 diagonal crisscross blocks. Trim the blocks to 8" x 8".

ASSEMBLING THE QUILT TOP

1. Arrange 56 of the blocks and two of the leftover 11" squares on point, referring to the quilt layout for the direction and placement of the blocks. Treat each block as if it were a half-square-triangle unit, paying close attention to the dark and light side of the blocks for correct placement.

2. Decide which of the leftover 11" squares you want in the center of the quilt and trim them down to 8" x 8". Replace them in the layout.

3. Look through a door peephole or use "The 10-Foot Rule" (page 5) to check the blending and separation from one color to the next. Switch the blocks around until you're satisfied with their arrangement. Keep in mind the blocks were cut free form; therefore, the design is not perfectly symmetrical. That's part of the charm!

4. Add the red orange print side and corner setting triangles to the quilt layout.

5. Pin and sew the blocks and side setting triangles together in diagonal rows. Press the seam allowances in opposite directions from row to row so they will nestle together when you join the rows.

6. Pin and sew the rows together in six groups of two rows each. Combine the sections together into the right half and left half of the quilt top. Join the right and left sides. Press the seam allowances in one direction.

7. Trim and square up the quilt top, making sure to leave ¼" for the seam allowance beyond the block corners.

FINISHING YOUR QUILT

Refer to "Finishing the Quilt" beginning on page 10 as needed.

Oh Baby!

It's always so much fun to make a baby quilt out of soft, warm flannels. This quilt is a good-sized crib quilt that will be useful for several years as the little one grows.

fabric tips

Choose a group of flannels that somewhat blend together for a soft look. Using multiple colors allows the quilt to work for boys or girls. For a "girl" quilt, swap out the two blues for two additional pinks. A little bit of white in most of the prints, such as the different-sized polka dots, will give your quilt a whimsical look. Choose blue for the border for a boy or pink for a girl.

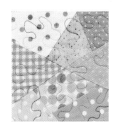

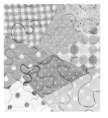

MATERIALS

⅞ yard of blue polka-dot flannel for border

⅜ yard *each* of 2 different blue print flannels for blocks

⅜ yard *each* of 2 different green print flannels for blocks

⅜ yard *each* of 2 multicolored print flannels for blocks

⅜ yard *each* of 1 pink print and 1 yellow print flannel for blocks

½ yard of fabric for binding

2⅞ yards of fabric for backing

48" x 64" piece of batting

CUTTING

From *each* of the 8 prints, cut:
1 strip, 11" x 42"; crosscut each strip into 3 squares, 11" x 11" (24 total). From 4 of the strips, cut an additional square, 7" x 7" (4 total)

From the blue polka-dot fabric, cut:
5 strips, 5" x 42"

From the binding fabric, cut:
6 strips, 2½" x 42"

MAKING THE BLOCKS

Refer to "Making the Crazy Blocks" on pages 6–9 for details as needed. Vary the number of A and B blocks as you prefer.

First cut

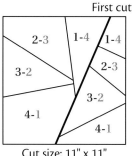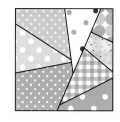

Cut size: 11" x 11"   Trimmed size: 8½" x 8½"
Block A

First cut

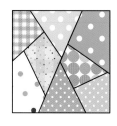

Cut size: 11" x 11"   Trimmed size: 8½" x 8½"
Block B

Cut size: 7" x 7"   Trimmed size: 5" x 5"
Corner block
Block cutting and sewing guide

1. Arrange the 11" squares into three decks of eight squares each. Each deck should contain eight different fabrics. Using the Block A and B diagrams, cut, shuffle, and secure each deck with a pin through all layers until ready to sew.
2. Make 24 eight-segment split blocks. Trim the blocks to 8½" x 8½".
3. Stack the four 7" squares into a deck. Using the corner block diagram, cut, shuffle, and secure the deck with a pin. Make four border corner blocks. Trim to 5" x 5".

ASSEMBLING THE QUILT TOP

1. Arrange the blocks into six horizontal rows of four blocks each.
2. Look through a door peephole or use "The 10-Foot Rule" (page 5) to check the balance of color. Switch and turn the blocks around until you're satisfied with their arrangement.
3. Sew the blocks together in horizontal rows and press seam allowances in opposite directions from row to row. Sew the rows together and press the seam allowances in one direction.
4. Sew the strips for the border together to make one long strip. Trim to the length and width of your quilt as directed in "Adding Borders" on page 10.
5. Sew the side borders to the quilt. Press the seam allowances toward the border strips.
6. Sew a corner block to each end of the top and bottom borders. Press seam allowances toward the border. Sew the borders to the top and bottom of the quilt; press.

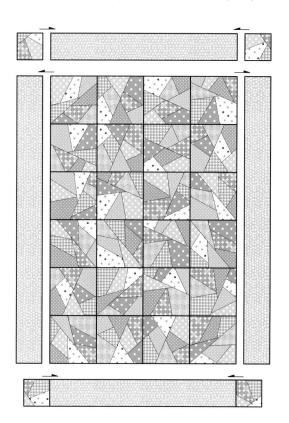

FINISHING YOUR QUILT

Refer to "Finishing the Quilt" beginning on page 10 as needed.

Finished quilt: 41½" x 57½" • Finished blocks: 8" x 8" and 4½" x 4½"

Blocks needed: 24 eight-segment split blocks and 4 four-segment split blocks

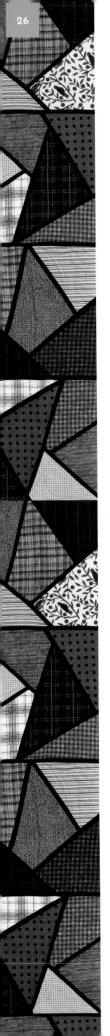

STAINED GLASS

The little black strips that I call "sticks" in the Crazy blocks create the look of lead in stained-glass windows. Adding strips is an easy technique and can be used for any of the Crazy blocks in this book. By adding strips, you can make as many cuts as you like, and your blocks will remain close to the size of your original squares. The strips fill in the space taken up by the seam allowances.

fabric tips

I went with a homespun theme for this quilt using flannels—plaids, polka-dot fabrics, striped fat quarters, and some tone-on-tone prints. I also added a print that had a bit of white in it for variety and to balance the other whites in the fabrics. It's important to use three or four with white rather than just one so the white is balanced. I also chose to make half the blocks with a five-segment cut and the other half with a six-segment cut. This changes the overall size of the segments from block A to block B, but the finished block size is the same. When the blocks are rather large, as they are here, having two different blocks adds more interest to the quilt. I'm anxious to try this pattern in batiks!

MATERIALS

3⅞ yards of black flannel for blocks, sashing, border, and binding

1 fat quarter *each* of 3 red plaid flannels for blocks

1 fat quarter *each* of 2 green print flannels for blocks

1 fat quarter *each* of 1 light green plaid and 1 light green checked flannel for blocks

1 fat quarter of 1 blue checked flannel for blocks

1 fat quarter of light print flannel for blocks

1 fat quarter of brown polka-dot flannel for blocks

1 fat quarter of gold plaid flannel for blocks

1 fat quarter of multicolored striped flannel for blocks

4⅝ yards of fabric for backing

65" x 81" piece of batting

CUTTING

From *each* of the 12 fat quarters, cut:
1 square, 17" x 17" (12 total)

From the fat quarters, cut a *total* of:
6 squares, 1" x 1"

From the black flannel, cut:
58 strips, 1" x 42"; from 34 of the strips, cut 17 pieces, 1" x 16"*
7 strips, 6½" x 42"
7 strips, 2½" x 42"
Wait until after the blocks are trimmed to cut the sashing pieces.

Finished quilt: 59" x 75" • Finished block: 15½" x 15½"
Blocks needed: 6 six-segment basic blocks (block A) and 6 five-segment basic blocks (block B)

MAKING THE BLOCKS

Refer to "Making the Crazy Blocks" on pages 6–9 for details as needed.

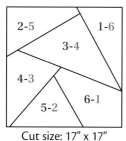
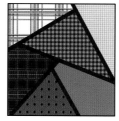

Cut size: 17" x 17"   Trimmed size: 16" x 16"

Block A

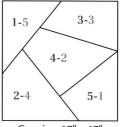
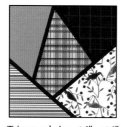

Cut size: 17" x 17"   Trimmed size: 16" x 16"

Block B

Block cutting and sewing guide

1. Arrange the 17" squares into two decks of six each. Each deck should contain six different fabrics. Make sure each deck has a good representation of each color. Cut one deck following the Block A diagram and one deck following the Block B diagram. Shuffle and secure the decks with a pin through all layers until ready to sew.

2. For the stained glass "lead" or what I call "sticks," you'll sew 1"-wide black strips to each cut edge before adding the next piece. Place a black strip over the cut edge of the first piece that you'll be sewing; trim the strip so that it's about 1" longer on each end. Align the raw edges and sew the strip to the first piece, right sides together. Press the seam allowances toward the black strip and trim the ends even with the first piece.

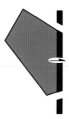

3. Follow the sewing order to align and sew the next cut piece to the black strip. Pin the strip first and open it out to make sure the edges are even with the previous piece. Continue in this manner to add black strips and block pieces until the block is complete. Trim the blocks to 16" x 16". You can trim your blocks to a larger or smaller size. Just be sure to trim them all to the same size. (Use the block size to cut the sashing strips.)

ASSEMBLING THE QUILT TOP

1. Arrange the blocks into four horizontal rows of three blocks each, alternating the A and B blocks as desired. Leave a space between the blocks for the sashing strips. Once you're satisfied with the layout, add the 1"-wide sashing strips and the 1" cornerstones.

2. Look through a door peephole or use "The 10-Foot Rule" (page 5) to check the balance of color. Switch and turn the blocks around until you're satisfied with their arrangement.

3. Sew the blocks and vertical sashing strips together into horizontal rows. Press the seam allowances toward the sashing strips. Make four rows, replacing them in the layout as you go.

4. Sew the horizontal sashing strips and cornerstones together into horizontal rows. Press the seam allowances toward the cornerstones. Make three rows, replacing them in the layout as you go.

5. Sew the sashing/cornerstone rows to the block/sashing rows. Press the seam allowances toward the sashing strips.

6. Sew the strips for the border together to make one long strip. Trim to size and sew to the quilt as directed in "Adding Borders" on page 10. Press the seam allowances toward the border strips.

FINISHING YOUR QUILT

Refer to "Finishing the Quilt" beginning on page 10 as needed.

ROLL OF THE DICE

The bright Crazy blocks in this quilt were a lot of fun to make. They took on an entirely different look when the sashing strips and pieced border were added. I like the clean-cut look of this quilt—the blocks appear to float atop a black-and-white checkerboard.

fabric tips

Search for a mix of bright colors for the Crazy blocks. I chose colors in pairs and made sure that each pair of colors was different enough from each other to provide contrast. Use the 10-foot rule to make sure the colors will go together yet be distinct from a distance.

MATERIALS

2 yards of white print for sashing and border

2 yards of black print for sashing and border

⅓ yard *each* of 2 blue prints for blocks

⅓ yard *each* of 2 turquoise prints for blocks

⅓ yard *each* of 2 green prints for blocks

⅓ yard *each* of 2 yellow prints for blocks

⅓ yard *each* of 2 red prints for blocks

⅓ yard *each* of 1 white print and 1 black print for blocks

⅝ yard of fabric for binding

5 yards of fabric for backing

64" x 83" piece of batting

CUTTING

From *each* of the 12 prints for blocks, cut:
1 strip, 9" x 42"; crosscut into 3 squares, 9" x 9" (36 total)

From the white print for sashing and border, cut:
5 strips, 3¼" x 42"
9 strips, 5¼" x 42"

From the black print for sashing and border, cut:
5 strips, 3¼" x 42"
9 strips, 5¼" x 42"

From the binding fabric, cut:
7 strips, 2½" x 42"

MAKING THE BLOCKS

Refer to "Making the Crazy Blocks" on pages 6–9 for details as needed. Vary the number of A and B blocks as you prefer.

First cut

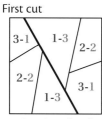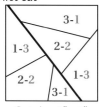

Cut size: 9" x 9"   Trimmed size: 6" x 6"

Block A

First cut

Cut size: 9" x 9"   Trimmed size: 6" x 6"

Block B

Block cutting and sewing guide

1. Arrange the 9" squares into six decks of six squares each. Each deck should contain six different prints. Cut, shuffle, and secure the decks with a pin through all layers until ready to sew.
2. Make 36 six-segment split blocks. Trim the blocks to 6" x 6". (You'll have one extra block.)

MAKING THE SASHING AND BORDERS

1. Sew the 3¼" white print and black print strips together in pairs to make five strip sets. Press the seam allowances toward the dark fabric. Crosscut the strip sets into 70 segments, 2½" wide.

2½"

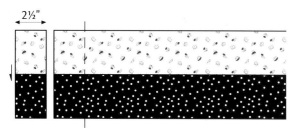

Make 5 strip sets.
Cut 70 segments.

2. Sew two of the segments from step 1 together as shown. Press the seam allowances to one side. Make 30. Set aside the remaining ten 2½" segments.

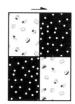

Make 30.

3. Sew the 5¼"-wide white print and black print strips together in pairs to make nine strip sets. Press seam allowances toward the dark fabric.

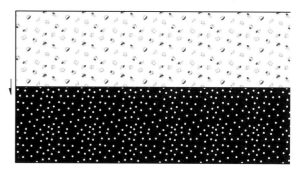

Make 5 strip sets.

4. Crosscut five of the strip sets into 70 segments, 2½" wide. Crosscut four strip sets into 26 segments, 5¼" wide.

2½"   5¼"

Cut 70 segments.   Cut 26 segments.

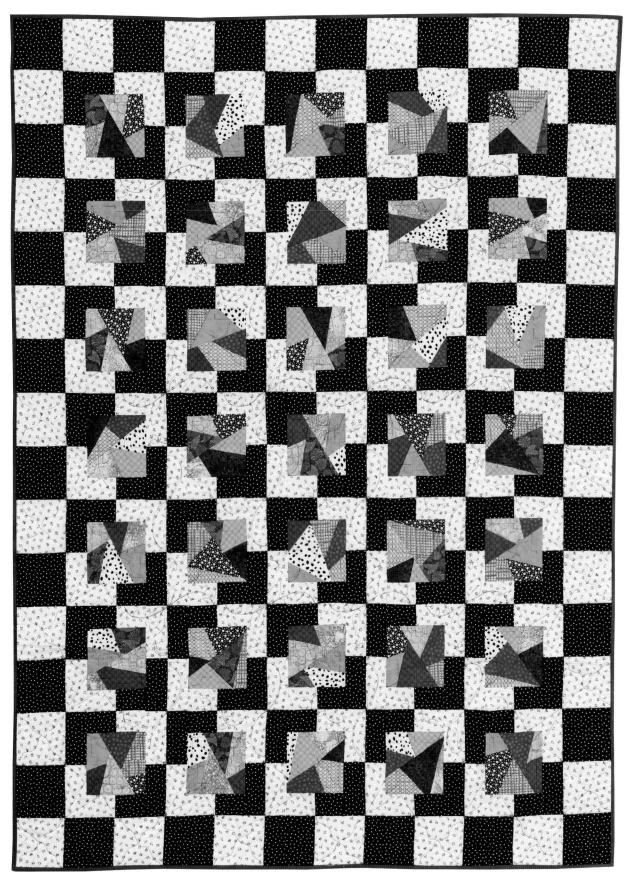

Finished quilt: 57½" x 76½" • Finished block: 5½" x 5½" • Blocks needed: 35 six-segment split blocks

5. Sew seven of the 2½"-wide sections together along the short ends to make one long vertical pieced sashing. Make 10 pieced sashing strips.

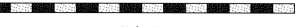

Make 10.

6. Sew the 5¼" segments together along the short ends, alternating the black and white prints. Make two strips with six segments each and two strips with seven segments each. Press seam allowances toward the dark fabric.

Make 2.

Make 2.

ASSEMBLING THE QUILT TOP

1. Arrange the Crazy blocks into seven horizontal rows of five blocks each, leaving space between the blocks for the sashing. Add the shorter pieced sashing sections between the blocks and add the 10 leftover sections from step 2 of "Making the Sashing and Borders" to the top and bottom of each row as shown. Add the long pieced sashing strips as shown in the quilt-layout diagram.

2. Look through a door peephole or use "The 10-Foot Rule" (page 5) to check the balance of color for the Crazy blocks. Switch and turn the blocks around until you're satisfied with their arrangement.

3. Sew the horizontal sashing between the blocks to make five vertical rows. Press seam allowances toward the sashing. Replace the rows in the layout as they're completed.

4. Pin and sew the long pieced sashing strips to the two outer rows, matching the seam intersections. Press the seam allowances toward the sashing strips. Replace the rows in the layout.

5. Pin and sew the remaining eight long pieced sashing strips together in pairs.

6. Pin and sew a long pieced sashing unit from step 5 on both sides of rows two and four. Press the seam allowances toward the Crazy blocks. Sew the rows together. Press the seam allowances toward the Crazy blocks.

7. Add the pieced borders with seven segments to the sides of the quilt. Press the seam allowances toward the border. Add the pieced borders with six segments to the top and bottom of the quilt. Press the seam allowances toward the border.

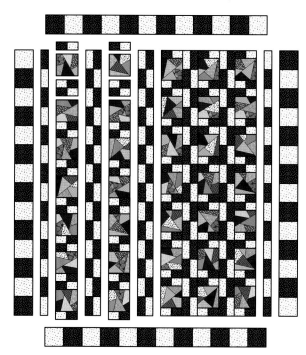

FINISHING YOUR QUILT

Refer to "Finishing the Quilt" beginning on page 10 as needed.

CURRY

Curry is a fun mix of some of my favorite reds. The cream fabric frames each block and separates one from the other. This stark contrast between the cream and the red makes each block a focal point of the design. I would like to try this design in another color, or combine a variety of colors, using one color per block.

fabric tips

To choose the fabrics for this quilt, I strongly suggest using my 10-foot rule. I chose reds and red oranges that were tone-on-tone prints with lots of movement in the print. I also made sure that they looked different from each other. Up close, the reds looked different, but when I used the 10-foot rule, many appeared too similar. I was able to replace the similar fabrics and add others that may have looked too orange, too dark, or otherwise too different when viewed up close.

MATERIALS

3⅜ yards of cream tone-on-tone print for block borders and outer border

⅓ yard *each* of 9 different tone-on-tone red and orange prints for Crazy blocks

1 yard of red print for sashing

⅛ yard of light orange print for cornerstones

⅔ yard of red print for binding

5 yards fabric for backing

69" x 90" piece of batting

CUTTING

From *each* of the 9 tone-on-tone red and orange prints, cut:

1 strip, 9" x 42"; crosscut into 4 squares, 9" x 9" (36 total)

From the cream print, cut:

30 strips, 2½" x 42"; crosscut into:
   70 rectangles, 2½" x 6"
   70 rectangles, 2½" x 10"
7 strips, 5" x 42"

From the red print for sashing, cut:

21 strips, 1½" x 42"; crosscut into 82 rectangles, 1½" x 10"

From the light orange print, cut:

2 strips, 1½" x 42"; crosscut into 48 squares, 1½" x 1½"

From the red print for binding, cut:

8 strips, 2½" x 42"

MAKING THE BLOCKS

Refer to "Making the Crazy Blocks" on pages 6–9 for details as needed. Vary the number of A and B blocks as you prefer.

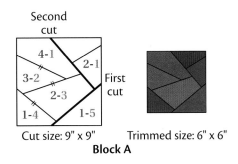

Cut size: 9" x 9"   Trimmed size: 6" x 6"
Block A

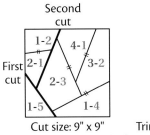

Cut size: 9" x 9"   Trimmed size: 6" x 6"
Block B

Block cutting and sewing guide

1. Arrange the 9" squares into five decks of seven squares each. Each deck should contain seven different prints. You will have one extra square. Cut, shuffle, and secure the decks with a pin through all layers until ready to sew.
2. Make 35 seven-segment blocks. Trim the blocks to 6" x 6".
3. Sew cream print 2½" x 6" rectangles to the sides of each block. Press the seam allowances toward the blocks. Sew cream print 2½" x 10" rectangles to the top and bottom of each block. Press the seam allowances toward the blocks.

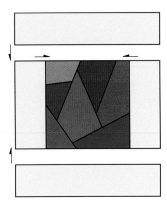

Make 35.

ASSEMBLING THE QUILT TOP

1. Arrange the blocks into seven horizontal rows of five blocks each, leaving a space between the blocks for the sashing. Look through a door peephole or use "The 10-Foot Rule" (page 5) to check the balance of color. Switch and turn the blocks around until you're satisfied with their arrangement. Add the red sashing strips and light orange cornerstones to the layout.
2. Sew the blocks and vertical sashing strips together into horizontal rows. Press the seam allowances toward the sashing strips. Make seven rows, replacing them in the layout as you go.
3. Sew the strips for the horizontal sashing and cornerstones together to make eight long strips as shown. Replace in the layout.
4. Sew the block rows and long sashing strips together. Press seam allowances toward the sashing.
5. Sew the strips for the border together to make one long strip. Trim to size and sew to the quilt as directed in "Adding Borders" on page 10. Press the seam allowances toward the border strips.

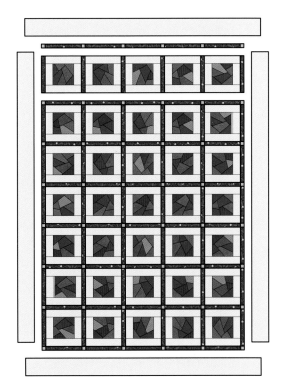

FINISHING YOUR QUILT

Refer to "Finishing the Quilt" beginning on page 10 as needed.

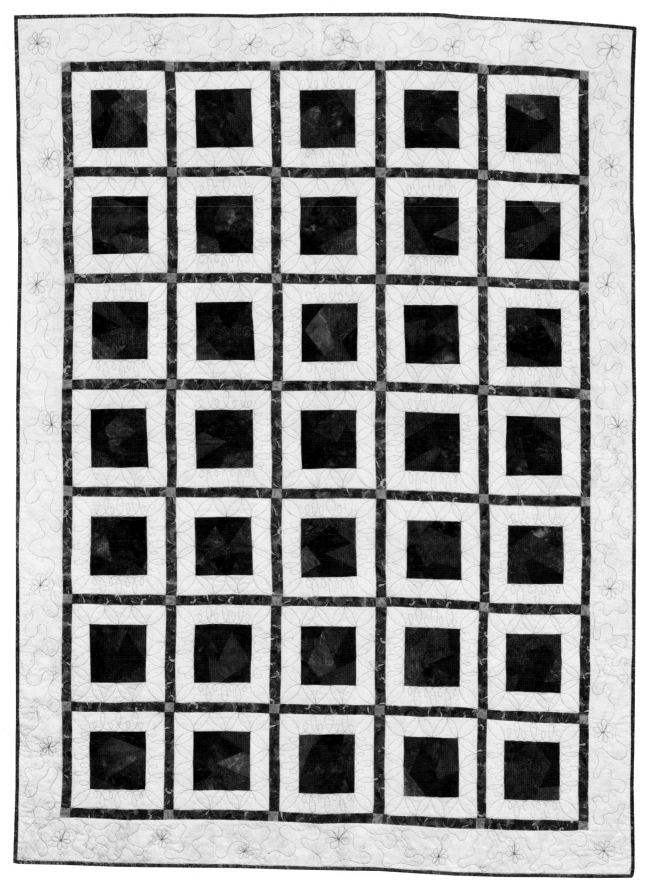

Finished quilt: 63" x 84" • Finished block: 5½" x 5½" • Blocks needed: 35 seven-segment multiple-unit blocks

Every Which Way

The first Crazy quilts were often made from bits and pieces of worn-out shirts and dresses. I wanted this quilt to look somewhat retro, using fabrics that could have been clothing in an earlier life. I also wanted to demonstrate how easily this method can be used with leftover fabrics. Slip in some fabrics from your stash and have fun!

fabric tips

Here's your chance to experiment with bold striped fabrics, polka-dot fabrics, graphic prints, and funky florals. But no matter what look you're seeking, choose a variety of prints that look very different from one another. Combine a mix of bold prints as well as simple tone-on-tone prints; then use the 10-foot rule to stand back and see if you like the mix. Have fun and be daring—throw in an unusual print or two!

MATERIALS

⅔ yard *each* of 2 brown, 2 red, 3 black, 2 turquoise, and 3 blue fabrics

1⅛ yards of dark gray print for outer border

1 yard of light print for sashing

½ yard of gold print for inner border

⅔ yard of fabric for binding

5 yards of fabric for backing

70" x 87" piece of batting

CUTTING

From *each* of the 12 prints for the blocks, cut:
2 squares, 11½" x 11½" (24 total)
2 squares, 9½" x 9½" (24 total)

From the light print, cut:
10 strips, 3" x 42"; crosscut into:
    24 rectangles, 3" x 6½"
    24 rectangles, 3" x 8½"

From the gold print, cut:
7 strips, 2" x 42"

From the dark gray print, cut:
7 strips, 5" x 42"

From the fabric for binding, cut:
8 strips, 2½" x 42"

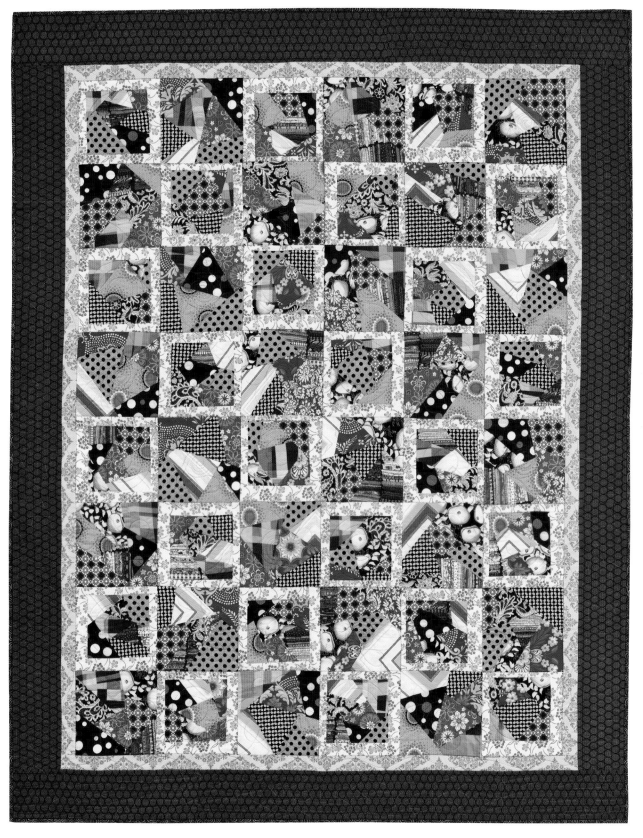

Finished quilt: 60½" x 76½" • Finished blocks: 6" x 6" and 8" x 8" • Blocks needed: 48 seven-segment multiple-unit blocks

MAKING THE BLOCKS

Refer to "Making the Crazy Blocks" on pages 6–9 for details as needed.

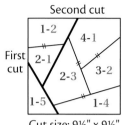

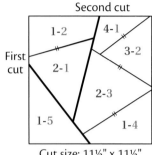
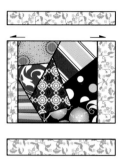

Second cut

First cut

1-2 4-1
2-1
2-3 3-2
1-5 1-4

Cut size: 9½" x 9½"   Trimmed size: 6½" x 6½"

Block A

Second cut

First cut

1-2 4-1
3-2
2-1
2-3
1-5 1-4

Cut size: 11½" x 11½"   Trimmed size: 8½" x 8½"

Block B

Block cutting and sewing guide

1. Arrange the 9½" squares into three decks of eight squares each. Likewise, arrange the 11½" squares into three decks of eight squares each. Each deck should contain eight different prints. Cut, shuffle, and secure the decks with a pin through all layers until ready to sew.

2. Make 24 seven-segment blocks from the 9½" squares and 24 seven-segment blocks from the 11½" squares. Trim the smaller blocks to 6½" x 6½" and trim the larger blocks to 8½" x 8½".

3. Neatly stack the 3" x 6½" sashing rectangles into four decks of six each. Cut lengthwise through the decks as shown to create two strips. The decks don't have to be cut exactly in half; just keep the minimum width on either side at least 1". Cut each deck differently from the last and keep the decks together. Stack and cut the 3" x 8½" sashing rectangles in the same way.

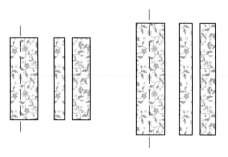

4. Sew the sashing rectangles from one side of a 6½"-long deck to the small Crazy blocks. Sew the remaining rectangles to the opposite side. Press seam allowances toward the sashing. Repeat for each deck. Then add the 8½"-long sashing rectangles to the top and bottom in the same way; press.

ASSEMBLING THE QUILT TOP

1. Arrange the blocks into eight horizontal rows of six blocks each, alternating the bordered blocks with the unbordered blocks. Switch and turn the blocks around until you're satisfied with their arrangement. Look through a door peephole or use "The 10-Foot Rule" (page 5) to check the balance of color and make changes as desired.

2. Sew the blocks together in rows. Press the seam allowances toward the bordered blocks. Sew the rows together in groups of two and press the seam allowances to one side. Finish sewing the rows together; then press seam allowances to one side.

3. Sew the gold strips for the inner border together to make one long strip. Trim to size and sew to the quilt as directed in "Adding Borders" on page 10. Press the seam allowances toward the border strips.

4. Repeat step 3 for the dark gray outer-border strips.

FINISHING YOUR QUILT

Refer to "Finishing the Quilt" beginning on page 10 as needed.

My Favorite Cords

I'm often asked if my Crazy quilt methods would work for heavy fabrics such as velvet, old jeans, and so on. I've already made a Crazy quilt out of velvet, so this time I decided to put the method to the test with corduroy. I had a great time mixing up different textures of corduroys, from pinwale to wide wale and everything in between. It was a blast to make, and it's sure to be a hit with the guys.

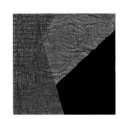

fabric tips

Look around in fabric stores that sell dressmaking material to find corduroys in your favorite colors. There is a wide variety of corduroy fabric. Don't let the nap scare you away from purchasing a color you love. Because the fabric is so thick, I used ½" seam allowances. Corduroy isn't the only option; you can also use velvet or lightweight denim.

MATERIALS

½ yard *each* of corduroy in 10 different solid colors for the blocks; I used black, blue, turquoise, green, olive, tan, dark brown, gray, gold, and burgundy

¾ yard of pinwale corduroy or cotton fabric for binding

4½ yards of pinwale corduroy or cotton fabric for backing*

51" x 73" piece of lightweight batting

*If you use cotton fabric or don't mind piecing the corduroy so that the grain runs horizontal on the back of the quilt, 3 yards of fabric is enough.

CUTTING

From *each* of the 10 corduroy fabrics for the blocks, cut:
1 strip, 15½" x 42"; cut into 2 squares, 15½" x 15½" (20 total)*

From the binding fabric, cut:
6 strips, 3" x 42"
*Save the remainder of the strips for the pieced border.

MAKING THE BLOCKS

Refer to "Making the Crazy Blocks" on pages 6–9 for details as needed.

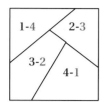

Cut size: 15½" x 15½"   Trimmed size: 12" x 12"
Block A

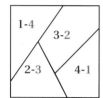

Cut size: 15½" x 15½"   Trimmed size: 12" x 12"
Block B

Block cutting and sewing guide

1. Arrange the 15½" squares into five decks of four squares each. Each deck should contain four different fabrics. Cut, shuffle, and secure the decks with a pin through all layers until ready to sew.
2. Make 20 four-segment whole blocks *using a ½" seam allowance*. Trim the blocks to 12" x 12".

ASSEMBLING THE QUILT TOP

1. Arrange the blocks into five horizontal rows of four blocks each. Look through a door peephole or use "The 10-Foot Rule" (page 5) to check the balance of color. Switch and turn the blocks around until you're satisfied with their arrangement.
2. Sew the blocks together in rows, again using a ½" seam allowance. Press the seam allowances open. Sew the rows together and press seam allowances open.
3. Stack the 10 strips (approximately 9" x 15½") left over from cutting the squares, into three decks, two with three fabrics each and one with four fabrics. Slice through each deck, making five cuts on two of the decks and four cuts on the remaining deck. Vary the widths, but cut all strips at least 1½" wide. Cut each deck differently.

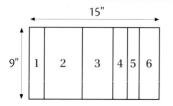

4. Sew the segments together randomly to make blocks of five or six fabrics each. Press the seam allowances open. Trim the top and bottom edges of each block to create a rectangle, 6½" long by whatever the width is.

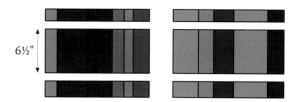

5. Mix the blocks up and sew into one long strip for the top and bottom borders. Refer to "Adding Borders" on page 10 to measure and trim the long strip into two borders. Sew them to the top and bottom edges of the quilt. Press the seam allowances open.

FINISHING YOUR QUILT

Refer to "Finishing the Quilt" beginning on page 10 as needed.

Finished quilt: 45" x 67" • Finished block: 11" x 11" • Blocks needed: 20 four-segment basic blocks

FIGS AND GINGER

I love the rich colors of fresh figs. Add the golden color of ginger, and it seemed a magical mix for a quilt! The combinations of batiks in earthy tones seemed perfect. And, of course batiks come in every color you can imagine to keep on making it better!

fabric tips

Check out your stash for fabrics to use in this quilt. There are six different colors, and you'll need anywhere from 12 to 24 squares of each. If you discover fabric that you can toss into the mix, even if it's just two or three pieces, go for it! I used all batiks and looked for small- to medium-scale prints with a lot of movement. As always, I used my 10-foot rule so that I didn't include prints that were too similar to each other.

MATERIALS

1½ yards of medium brown batik for border

⅓ yard *each* of 6 different gold batiks for blocks

⅓ yard *each* of 6 different red batiks for blocks

⅓ yard *each* of 6 different tan batiks for blocks

⅓ yard *each* of 6 different green batiks for blocks

⅓ yard *each* of 3 different medium brown batiks for blocks

⅓ yard *each* of 3 different dark brown batiks for blocks

⅔ yard of fabric for binding

5¼ yards of fabric for backing

68" x 90" piece of batting

CUTTING

From *each* of the gold, red, tan, and green batiks, cut:
1 strip, 9" x 42"; crosscut into 4 squares, 9" x 9"
    (24 squares of each color)

From *each* of the dark brown and medium brown batiks, cut:
1 strip, 9" x 42"; crosscut into 4 squares, 9" x 9"
    (12 squares of each color)

From the brown batik for the border, cut:
7 strips, 6½" x 42"

From the binding fabric, cut:
8 strips, 2½" x 42"

Finished quilt: 62" x 84" • Finished block: 5½" x 5½" • Blocks needed: 117 six-segment crisscross blocks

MAKING THE BLOCKS

Refer to "Making the Crazy Blocks" on pages 6–9 for details as needed.

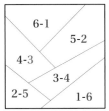

Cut size: 9" x 9"   Trimmed size: 6" x 6"

Block cutting and sewing guide

1. Arrange the 9" squares into decks of six fabrics each as follows: 4 decks of tan and green; 4 decks of gold and red; 2 decks of green and gold; 2 decks of red and medium brown; 2 decks of medium brown and green; 2 decks of tan and dark brown; 2 decks of dark brown and gold; 2 decks of red and tan. Use 6 different fabrics in each deck, and be sure to alternate the two colors in each stack. Cut, shuffle, and secure each deck with a pin through all layers until ready to sew.
2. Make 120 six-segment crisscross blocks. Trim the blocks to 6" x 6". Feel free to cut them larger if you can; there are no setting triangles or alternate blocks to worry about.

ASSEMBLING THE QUILT TOP

1. Arrange the blocks into 13 horizontal rows of nine blocks each. Refer to the quilt diagram at right for placement. Look through a door peephole or use "The 10-Foot Rule" (page 5) to check the balance of color. Switch and turn the blocks around until you're satisfied with their arrangement. You'll have three extra blocks.
2. Sew the blocks into rows. Press the seam allowances in opposite direction from row to row. Sew the rows together in six sets of two rows each. Press the seam allowances to one side. Sew the sets together; then add the last row. Press seam allowances to one side.

3. Sew the strips for the border together to make one long strip. Trim to size and sew to the quilt as directed in "Adding Borders" on page 10. Press the seam allowances toward the border strips.

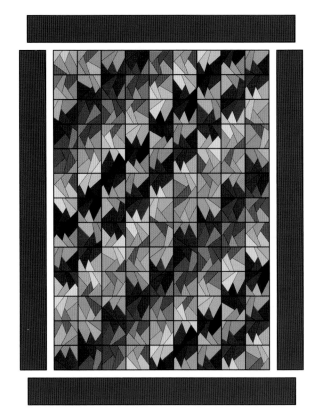

FINISHING YOUR QUILT

Refer to "Finishing the Quilt" beginning on page 10 as needed.

Scrappy Crazy Quilt Sampler

This scrappy sampler was made with two different-sized blocks, making it fun to work your quilt into an original design. Four small blocks sewn together total the same dimensions of the large block, providing a lot of different design possibilities for the layout. You can sew the small blocks into a four-patch unit using all light blocks, all dark blocks, or a combination of both. If you want to add another row or two to make your quilt larger, you can always add more 6½" solid squares to the mix until you get the size you want.

fabric tips

I wanted a bright, cheery, blended look for this quilt, so I was careful to choose fabrics in bright colors that have chunky, uneven designs. I also made sure each print had at least three different colors. Next I went about dividing my fabrics into two groups—medium light and medium dark. To keep a nice even flow, I used one of the same prints in both the light and dark groups. Because I love working from my stash of fabrics, you might notice a few more prints in the mix than what is listed in the fabric requirements. If you have a stash of fabric, I encourage you to do the same.

MATERIALS

⅝ yard *each* of 7 different multicolored medium-light prints

⅝ yard *each* of 7 different multicolored medium-dark prints

⅝ yard of fabric for binding

3¼ yards of fabric for backing

55" x 79" piece of batting

CUTTING

From *each* of the 7 medium-light prints, cut:*
1 square, 16½" x 16½" (7 total)
3 squares, 10¼" x 10¼" (21 total)

From the remainder of the medium-light prints, cut:
4 assorted squares, 6½" x 6½" (optional)

From *each* of the 7 medium-dark prints, cut:*
1 square, 15½" x 15½" (7 total)
3 squares, 9½" x 9½" (21 total)

From the remainder of the medium-dark prints, cut:
4 assorted squares, 6½" x 6½" (optional)

From the binding fabric, cut:
7 strips, 2½" x 42"
*Note: Cut the 16½" square first and do not cut a strip across the fabric or you may not have enough.

MAKING THE BLOCKS

Refer to "Making the Crazy Blocks" on pages 6–9 for details as needed.

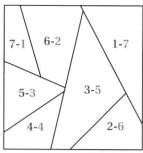

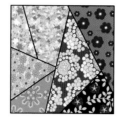

Cut size: 16½" x 16½"   Trimmed size: 12½" x 12½"

Block A

First cut

Cut size: Trimmed size:
10¼" x 10¼"   6½" x 6½"

Block B

Block cutting and sewing guide

1. Arrange the seven different 16½" medium-light squares in a deck. Cut, shuffle, and secure the deck with a pin through all layers until ready to sew.
2. Arrange the seven different 16½" medium-dark squares in a deck. Cut, shuffle, and secure the deck with a pin through all layers until ready to sew.
3. Make seven medium-light blocks and seven medium-dark blocks for a total of 14. Trim the blocks to 12½" x 12½".
4. Arrange the 10¼" medium-light squares in three decks of seven squares each. Each deck should contain seven different prints. Cut, shuffle, and secure each deck with a pin through all layers until ready to sew.
5. Arrange the 10¼" medium-dark squares in three decks of seven squares each. Each deck should contain seven different prints. Cut, shuffle, and secure each deck with a pin through all layers until ready to sew.
6. Make 21 medium-light blocks and 21 medium-dark blocks. Trim the blocks to 6½" x 6½".

ASSEMBLING THE QUILT TOP

1. There are many options when laying out the blocks for this quilt. You can use all of the small Crazy quilt blocks, in which case you'll have an extra dark and light block left over. Or, you can substitute some of the optional 6½" fabric squares for some of the small Crazy blocks. I swapped five medium-light and four medium-dark squares in place of the pieced light and dark blocks. (That meant I had 11 extra blocks to use in another project or on the back of the quilt.) You can also use all the pieced blocks and add in plain squares to make your quilt larger. View your arrangement through a door peephole or use "The 10-foot Rule" (page 5) to check the visual balance.
2. Sew the small blocks into two-patch and four-patch units as shown or as needed for your layout. Press the seam allowances toward the solid blocks or the dark blocks.
3. Sew the blocks into rows and sections as shown in the quilt assembly diagram. Press seam allowances toward the large blocks when possible.

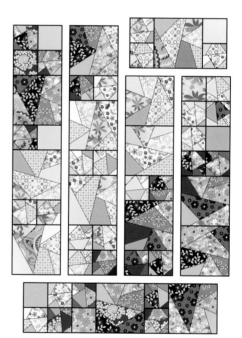

FINISHING YOUR QUILT

Refer to "Finishing the Quilt" beginning on page 10 as needed.

Finished quilt: 48½" x 72½" • Finished blocks: 12" x 12" and 6" x 6"
Blocks needed: 14 seven-segment whole blocks and 32 seven-segment split blocks

About the Author

Karla Alexander—quiltmaker, teacher, and author—has written five previous books; this is her sixth book on the art of quiltmaking. Karla has contributed her designs to Martingale & Company's yearly wall calendars, the *Creative Quilt Collection Volume Two* (2007), as well as *Skinny Quilts and Table Runners II* (2009).

She has also developed her own quilt-design business, Saginaw Street Quilt Company, which offers a line of more than 50 different designs in addition to a line of ruler designs with Creative Grid Rulers. The rulers work well with many of her books as well as new patterns. She enjoys creating designs that enable the maker to reason out the cuts and placement of blocks for themselves, making the final result truly unique to each quilter. Karla also believes that beautiful doesn't have to be difficult, and she specializes in techniques that are doable to the average or beginning quilter with just some good old-fashioned practice.

Karla lives in Salem, Oregon, with her husband, Don; the youngest of their three sons, William; and Lucy, the almost-black Lab.

THERE'S MORE ONLINE!

Visit Karla's quilt-design business at www.saginawstreetquilts.com. For more great books on quilting, visit www.martingale-pub.com.